Jim Peal, Ph.D

CHECK YOUR ATTITUDE

WORKBOOK

© Copyright 2016 by Jim Peal, Ph.D.

ISBN 978-1533334459

Published by Leadership Development Group, Oakland CA Tel. (01) 805-966-3323

What's your attitude got to do with it?

We have all been around someone with a crappy attitude.

While research proves what we all know about the impact of attitude on performance, if unchecked, negative energy becomes a contagion that sweeps through your office eroding creativity, productivity and ultimately the bottom line.

Don't be that person with a crappy attitude!

Check Your Attitude Instead.

Check Your Tude Table

At a glance you can see the negative and positive mindsets that typically come up at work and in your life along with tips on how to change negative attitudes into positive ones and how to enhance your positive strength attitudes.

The Check Your Tude website, www.checkyourtude.biz, the Apple or Android Check Your Tude apps ae easy to understand and use. The website and Business version of the apps have built in neuro-science conditioning tools, Maximize Your Strengths and Winning Formula that help you build the positive mental patterns that lead to a productive life.

This handy guidebook is an owner's manual that points out where the controls are so that you can adjust your own attitude. In no time you will learn how to recognize, realize, resolve and choose your attitudes. You'll learn to see where you are coming from and the impact you are having and make the course adjustments to keep work and life on track.

Table of Contents

Attitudes Index   5

CHECK YOUR TUDE®

What mindset are you operating from?

MINDSET

LEADERSHIP

DRAMA

EVENTS / ISSUES / CHALLENGES

DRAMA
Negative Intention

- Looks for what is wrong
- Finds fault
- Sees self as superior
- Invalidates & insults
- Interrupts & dominates
- Hostility
- Critical
- Withdraws energy
- Withholds information
- Sabotages

LEADERSHIP
Positive Intention

- Assumes the best
- Curious — asks questions
- Sees multiple perspectives
- Listens generously
- Adds energy
- Picks up on key points and expands them
- Supports & validates
- Builds trust
- Seeks common ground and accepts differences

Communication Loops

Our loops interact with each other to either build or erode trust.

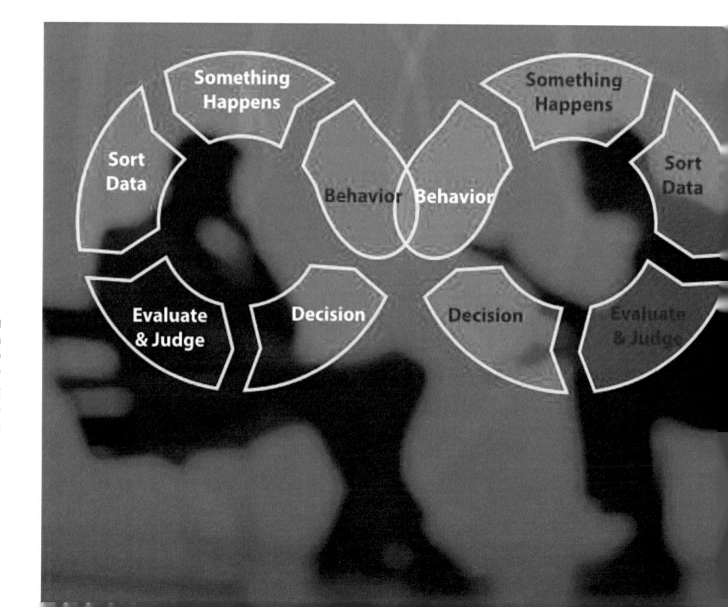

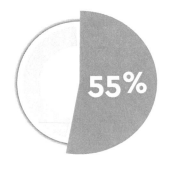

Digital — Words   **Analog** — How words are spoken   **Analog** — Body language

Emotional Contagion

Emotions and attitudes are spread rapidly through your non-verbal behavior, your analog. Most of the time your non-verbal behavior is in your blind spot.

CHECK YOUR TUDE®

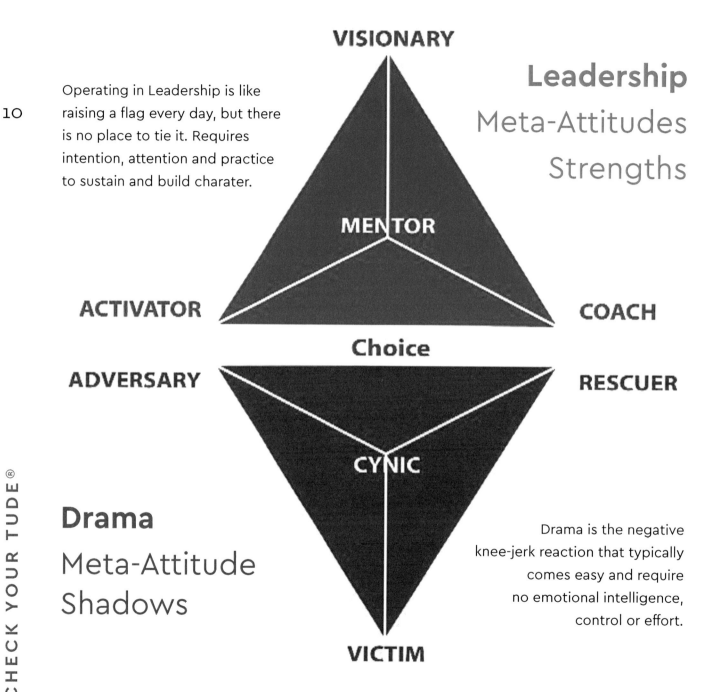

10

Operating in Leadership is like raising a flag every day, but there is no place to tie it. Requires intention, attention and practice to sustain and build charater.

VISIONARY

Leadership
Meta-Attitudes
Strengths

MENTOR

ACTIVATOR

COACH

Choice

ADVERSARY

RESCUER

CYNIC

Drama

Meta-Attitude
Shadows

Drama is the negative knee-jerk reaction that typically comes easy and require no emotional intelligence, control or effort.

VICTIM

Check Your Tude®

Sb Sabotage										Sv Service
Vt Victim	**Re** Resigned	**Sp** Suspicious	**En** Envious	**Df** Defensive	**In** Inspired	**Cr** Creative	**Cu** Curious	**Cm** Committed	**Vi** Visionary	
Ad Adversary	**Bl** Blaming	**Sr** Sarcastic	**Ag** Angry	**Fs** Frustrated	**Eg** Engaged	**Pa** Passionate	**Hu** Humorous	**Ac** Accountable	**Av** Activator	
Rs Rescuer	**Su** Superior	**Cn** Controlling	**Ha** Hidden Agenda	**Ar** Arrogant	**Hm** Humble	**Tp** Transparent	**Tr** Trusting	**Sp** Supportive	**Co** Coach	
Cy Cynic	**Sk** Skeptical	**Ct** Critical	**Is** Insulted	**Jg** Judgmental	**Ap** Accepting	**Cf** Confident	**Ob** Objective	**Md** Mindful	**Mn** Mentor	

Negative Intention Shadows — Choice — Positive Intention Strengths

Organization of the chart

The chart looks like a chemistry periodic table of the elements but consists of mindsets as the elements.

Service or Sabotage is the ultimate outcome when you choose

Positive or Negative intention as the basis for your mindset.

The outside columns represent the Meta-Attitudes for that row.

The inside elements are arranged symmetrically across from each other.

If you are in the red, look across the row to the same place in the green, where you will see an obvious place (not the only place) to go to be more effective at work and happier in your relationships and life.

If you want to strengthen a positive quality you can look first in the same column; otherwise, pick one strength from each row to help balance your strengths. You will see the symmetrical pairs of attitudes in this guide at a glance.

Notes

. . . .

. . . .

. . . .

. . . .

. . . .

. . . .

. . . .

. . . .

. . . .

. . . .

. . . .

. . . .

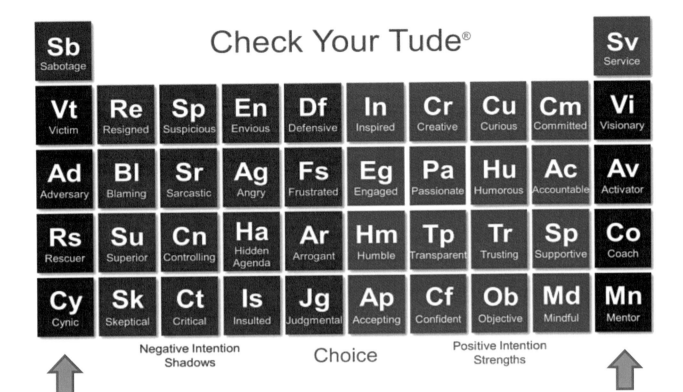

Check Your Tude®

| Sb Sabotage | | | | | | | | | | Sv Service |

| Vt Victim | Re Resigned | Sp Suspicious | En Envious | Df Defensive | In Inspired | Cr Creative | Cu Curious | Cm Committed | Vi Visionary |

| Ad Adversary | Bl Blaming | Sr Sarcastic | Ag Angry | Fs Frustrated | Eg Engaged | Pa Passionate | Hu Humorous | Ac Accountable | Av Activator |

| Rs Rescuer | Su Superior | Cn Controlling | Ha Hidden Agenda | Ar Arrogant | Hm Humble | Tp Transparent | Tr Trusting | Sp Supportive | Co Coach |

| Cy Cynic | Sk Skeptical | Ct Critical | Is Insulted | Jg Judgmental | Ap Accepting | Cf Confident | Ob Objective | Md Mindful | Mn Mentor |

Negative Intention Shadows — Choice — Positive Intention Strengths

The Meta Attitudes

Lead to Sabotage or Service

The Meta-Attitudes are the large categories of attitudes. They represent the attitudes of the samecolor in that row.It works best to operate from a combination of positive attitudes, at least one from each green row, to balance your strengths. Operating from just one strength lends itself to exaggerate the shadow of that strength. Balancing your strengths enhances the positive impact of your strengths

A **Victim** gives up because they are certain the negative in the past will become their future and they are helpless to change their circumstances.

The **Visionary** inspires by creating an experience of the future that is palpable, filled with passion and excitement for what is ahead.

Drama					Leadership				
Vt Victim	**Re** Resigned	**Sp** Suspicious	**En** Envious	**Df** Defensive	**In** Inspired	**Cr** Creative	**Cu** Curious	**Cm** Committed	**Vi** Visionary
Ad Adversary	**Bl** Blaming	**Sr** Sarcastic	**Ag** Angry	**Fs** Frustrated	**Eg** Engaged	**Pa** Passionate	**Hu** Humorous	**Ac** Accountable	**Av** Activator
Rs Rescuer	**Su** Superior	**Cn** Controlling	**Ha** Hidden Agenda	**Ar** Arrogant	**Hm** Humble	**Tp** Transparent	**Tr** Trusting	**Sp** Supportive	**Co** Coach
Cy Cynic	**Sk** Skeptical	**Ct** Critical	**Is** Insulted	**Jg** Judgmental	**Ap** Accepting	**Cf** Confident	**Ob** Objective	**Md** Mindful	**Mn** Mentor

Negative Intention Shadows   Choice   Positive Intention Strengths

Notes

. . . .

. . . .

. . . .

. . . .

. . . .

. . . .

. . . .

. . . .

. . . .

. . . .

. . . .

. . . .

Vt

Victim

[**vik**-tim]

1. **You blame outside circumstances for your situation.**
2. **You do not see yourself as powerful.**
3. **You have excuses for everything.**
4. **You gossip rather than talk with the person directly.**

RECOGNIZE
YOUR THOUGHTS, FEELINGS & ENERGY

1. "It is hopeless and I am helpless."
2. "I can't..."
3. "I have no power here."
4. "I have tried, but I keep getting blocked."
5. "It's no use."
6. "Do you know what _____ did to me?"

You feel defeated by external circumstances. Your energy seems to have vanished and you have lost all confidence in making a difference.

REALIZE
WHAT IS DRIVING YOUR MINDSET

1. You have betrayed your own value and your own worth but you think it is someone else's fault for your feeling.
2. You project all the positive qualities outside of yourself and internalize the negative.
3. You think your energy away by not recognizing or acknowledging your own power—this creates a black hole.
4. Giving up is your first thought.
5. You feel that you have no control but you have given up.
6. You feel betrayed – wronged or violated – by people's actions and lack of consideration.
7. You have a lot of unspoken rules and a lot of unspoken lines that get crossed.
8. You are like the kid who goes limp when you want to pick him up.
9. Your need for approval, for acknowledgment, for recognition, is never satisfied.
10. You drain people.
11. You are drained of energy because you don't have a strong enough core of positive thoughts about yourself.

RESOLVE
TO MOVE FORWARD

1. Own the fact that you have given up on yourself and that you can't expect someone to make up for your lack of self-worth; only you can make yourself whole.
2. Do a review of your strengths. Write them down.
3. Take action toward your goals even if they are small steps.
4. Identify where you give your power away to a person or situation. What would happen if you didn't? Start taking action in that direction.
5. Identify the shoulds, can'ts, and have-to's you always say. What rules or false beliefs keep you stuck?
6. Begin to say "I want to" or "I choose not to" instead of "I can't."
7. Have the conversation with whomever you have issues with rather than gossip about them.
8. Forgive those who you think have betrayed you. Forgiveness is giving up your right for revenge forever.
9. Recognize that you are, at your core, good.

Vi

Visionary

[**vizh**-*uh*-ner-ee]

1. having or showing clear ideas about what should happen or be done in the future
2. motivated & energized by the vision
3. in the face of challenges you keep the focus on the goal

RECOGNIZE
YOUR THOUGHTS, FEELINGS & ENERGY

1. "I am inspired and excited by what I see is possible."
2. "I see a world that works better than it does now."
3. "Obstacles are only temporary."
4. "You can count on me to follow through."
5. "His/her reputation is sterling."
6. You are excited and on fire about your vision. You are focused. You rally the troops. Because you are clear and committed, people trust you.

You are excited and on fire about your vision. You are focused. You rally the troops. Because you are clear and committed, people trust you.

REALIZE
WHAT IS DRIVING YOUR MINDSET

1. You have a visceral feeling about the vision. It registers in the core of your body as a deep sense of confidence. The vision has a three-dimensional quality to it that makes it very real.
2. You are focused on the course and direction.
3. You see the interrelatedness of things.
4. You feel the outreaching possibilities of the vision and how this vision interconnects with other people, systems and organizations.
5. You are at the 50,000-foot level and see the big picture, 360 degrees around.
6. You exude an appreciation for what is around you.
7. You recognize the value in each person, each component, and your attitude is one of inclusion.
8. You create an environment everyone wants to inhabit.
9. You know how to engage and invite all the different elements and personalities into the whole so that they can interact in a productive way.
10. You don't live in denial, you acknowledge the obstacles that arise and consistently keep everyone focused on where you are going.
11. Because you are congruent in your speech and actions you instill trust in those around you.
12. You are living and breathing that future vision.
13. You bring a sense of inspiration because you build a window into the future that is palpable, filled with passion and excitement for what is to become.

RESOLVE
TO BALANCE YOUR STRENGTHS

1. Allow your vision to mature.
2. Once you get the picture, focus on the details of closing the gap and getting there.
3. Take time to explain so that everyone knows the path forward and how progress will be measured.
4. Support people in their day-to-day tasks.
5. Stay awake and mindful of what is going on around you with people and processes. Respond and focus as things change.
6. Speak your vision freely; engage concerns and questions from those around you. It is normal for people to doubt. Help them see their way forward. Stay the course.
7. Ask people what's in it for them and link their drivers to the vision.
8. Validate, acknowledge and celebrate the small steps forward.

CHECK YOUR TUDE ®

The **Adversary** uses their anger to bully, intimidate and threaten in order to get their way.

The **Activator** instills a sense of urgency as they architect processes, identify roles and responsibilities, milestones, and action timelines to take us from where we are today to the vision of tomorrow.

Drama   **Leadership**

Vt	Re	Sp	En	Df	In	Cr	Cu	Cm	Vi
Victim	Resigned	Suspicious	Envious	Defensive	Inspired	Creative	Curious	Committed	Visionary

Ad	Bl	Sr	Ag	Fs	Eg	Pa	Hu	Ac	Av
Adversary	Blaming	Sarcastic	Angry	Frustrated	Engaged	Passionate	Humorous	Accountable	Activator

Rs	Su	Cn	Ha	Ar	Hm	Tp	Tr	Sp	Co
Rescuer	Superior	Controlling	Hidden Agenda	Arrogant	Humble	Transparent	Trusting	Supportive	Coach

Cy	Sk	Ct	Is	Jg	Ap	Cf	Ob	Md	Mn
Cynic	Skeptical	Critical	Insulted	Judgmental	Accepting	Confident	Objective	Mindful	Mentor

Negative Intention
Shadows

Choice

Positive Intention
Strengths

Notes

. . . .

. . . .

. . . .

. . . .

. . . .

. . . .

. . . .

. . . .

. . . .

. . . .

. . . .

. . . .

Adversary

[**ad**-ver-ser-ee]

1. You see yourself as doing it right while everyone else is doing it wrong.
2. You are always irritated at other people's shortcomings. You say, "Yes, but..."
3. You blame. You rarely step into other people's shoes to see their side of things.

RECOGNIZE
YOUR THOUGHTS, FEELINGS & ENERGY

1. "I know I am right and you are wrong."
2. "It is your/their fault these mistakes happened."
3. "The other team dropped the ball."
4. "I have to work with these imbeciles."
5. "If you weren't so stupid, you would understand this."

You are determined. You are mentally and emotionally calm and assured.

REALIZE
WHAT IS DRIVING YOUR MINDSET

1. You make people feel pressured, attacked, intimidated, and just plain wrong and then blame them for feeling that way.
2. You focus on what is wrong.
3. You point the finger and are very critical, looking for who is at fault.
4. You acknowledge what is wrong but don't acknowledge anything positive.
5. You put yourself in a one-up position.
6. You come off as condescending, with an inflated self-image, and are often seen as arrogant.
7. Your one-up position supports your anger about how inferior the world is around you.
8. You are always looking outside of yourself for fault because you see yourself as faultless.
9. You express their hostility directly or often through sarcasm.
10. You will take a defensive posture when criticized or asked to take responsibility.

RESOLVE
TO MOVE FORWARD

1. Realize that your attitude is creating the biggest part of the problem. Admit that you are not open-minded.
2. Step into others' shoes and feel how your negativity impacts them.
3. Let other people be right. Argue their position rather than against them.
4. It is not up to others to step up; it is up to you to create a safe space.
5. Coach others instead of criticizing them.
6. Accept that you are choosing being right over choosing what is true.
7. Think of the positives and mention them.
8. Identify what you are afraid might happen. Identify where you feel helpless.
9. What do you want for yourself? for others?
10. Where do you blame others rather than taking responsibility?
11. Make fun of yourself.
12. Notice where you use sarcasm rather than offering a constructive comment.
13. Acknowledge people twice as much as you criticize them.

Activator

[**ak**-t*uh*-vey-ter]

1. You love organizing and getting people moving toward the goal.
2. You live by your timelines. You get results.
3. You are accountable and hold people accountable in a way that motivates them.
4. You don't mind rocking the boat to get things moving.

RECOGNIZE
YOUR THOUGHTS, FEELINGS & ENERGY

1. "Let's get this show on the road!"
2. "OK, is everyone clear on what they will be doing?"
3. "We are making progress."
4. "Let's step out of our boxes and create a new way to work."
5. "We are going to hit our targets."

You are determined and energized, seeing possibilities in all situations.

REALIZE
WHAT IS DRIVING YOUR MINDSET

1. Architecting process and identifying roles and responsibilities, milestones and action timelines get you excited.
2. You bring forth a sense of urgency by having one foot firmly in the reality of today to pull it forward and one foot in the vision of tomorrow providing the pathway, the steps, to strategize and be the communicator to bring people forward.
3. You are very pragmatic and concrete.
4. You are always working toward the goal with relaxed zest.
5. Your positive energy favorably affects the people and working environment. You get things to happen.
6. You are a transformative energizer for individuals, groups and projects.
7. Your mindset answers the question, "How are we going to get there?"

RESOLVE
TO BALANCE YOUR STRENGTHS

1. Create a plan and follow through until it's complete.
2. Focus on the details of getting there. Make sure everyone knows the path forward and how progress will be measured.
3. Support people in their day-to-day tasks.
4. Stay awake and mindful of what is going on around you with people and processes. Respond and focus as things change.
5. Speak your vision freely; engage concerns and questions from those around you. It is normal for people to doubt. Help them see their way forward. Stay the course.
6. Ask people what's in it for them and link their drivers to the vision.
7. Validate, acknowledge and celebrate the small steps forward.

CHECK YOUR TUDE ®

The **Rescuer** takes over rather than teach and empower others.

The **Coach** directly and respectfully engages you in powerful ways to bring forth your strengths and capabilities in your day-to-day activities.

Drama **Leadership**

Vt	Re	Sp	En	Df	In	Cr	Cu	Cm	Vi
Victim	Resigned	Suspicious	Envious	Defensive	Inspired	Creative	Curious	Committed	Visionary

Ad	Bl	Sr	Ag	Fs	Eg	Pa	Hu	Ac	Av
Adversary	Blaming	Sarcastic	Angry	Frustrated	Engaged	Passionate	Humorous	Accountable	Activator

Rs	Su	Cn	Ha	Ar	Hm	Tp	Tr	Sp	Co
Rescuer	Superior	Controlling	Hidden Agenda	Arrogant	Humble	Transparent	Trusting	Supportive	Coach

Cy	Sk	Ct	Is	Jg	Ap	Cf	Ob	Md	Mn
Cynic	Skeptical	Critical	Insulted	Judgmental	Accepting	Confident	Objective	Mindful	Mentor

Negative Intention
Shadows

Choice

Positive Intention
Strengths

Notes

. . . .

. . . .

. . . .

. . . .

. . . .

. . . .

. . . .

. . . .

. . . .

. . . .

. . . .

. . . .

Rescuer

[**res**-kyoo-r]

1. **You take over rather than teach. You see yourself as the only one who is capable.**
2. **You listen to people complain about the same things over and over.**
3. **You think the project, work, business would fall apart if you were not there.**

RECOGNIZE
YOUR THOUGHTS, FEELINGS & ENERGY

1. "If I weren't here this place would fall apart."
2. "He really needs my help."
3. "Sure is a good thing I arrived when I did."
4. "They sure are trying soooo hard."
5. "They just don't seem to understand how to get this done."

You are determined. You are mentally and emotionally calm and assured.

REALIZE
WHAT IS DRIVING YOUR MINDSET

1. You see the world as a place that needs your salvation.
2. You want to appear like you just want to "help," but underneath your seeming kindness is an active subtext that says, "I am helping you because you don't have what it takes and I do."
3. You minimize the other person's power, effectiveness, skills and talents.
4. You are on the hunt for what is missing, but only if what is missing is what you have to offer.
5. You hold a judgment of others as being inadequate and incapable.
6. Unlike the Adversary, who will sit on the sidelines and criticize, you will not hesitate to jump right onto the playing field, take over, and take all the credit.
7. You elevate yourself in the presence of the Victim and validate the Victim's thought that they are helpless and the situation is hopeless but you will save the day.
8. You look like a team player but you are there to hijack the credit.
9. You will give you a false sense of hope but really you disempower people.

RESOLVE
TO MOVE FORWARD

1. Create situations where you teach rather than take over.
2. If you take on a task for someone, set up a time to teach the person how to do the task.
3. When a person repeats the same old story again, stop them and ask, "What do you want in this situation? What are you going to do to move in that direction?"
4. When you help someone out, let go of any expectation to be acknowledged for helping.
5. Stop from automatically volunteering your time. Ask yourself if you really have the time or energy to freely take on the task.
6. Understand that letting people struggle with a problem can be a great learning opportunity for them.
7. Realize that selfless service is different from rescuing – the true spirit of giving is without expectation for return.

Coach

[kohch]

1. **Help people become capable and confident.**
2. **See their inner strengths, potential and capabilities.**
3. **Create the environment and stimulation so you can be your best and really shine.**

RECOGNIZE
YOUR THOUGHTS, FEELINGS & ENERGY

1. "I see you as a strong and capable person and will not settle for less from you."
2. "Here are the strengths I see in you..."
3. "I know you can do it."
4. "These are the three things you try out to see what works the best for you."
5. "Here is how I see you shooting yourself in the foot."

The Visionary creates the vision, the Activator plots the course to get there, and the Coach is there beside you to encourage you to be your best as you work toward the goals.

REALIZE
WHAT IS DRIVING YOUR MINDSET

1. A Coach does not force you into anything. A Coach provides the tools for development, and while this process may have its moments of discomfort, embarrassment and hard work, a Coach does not shy away because a Coach believes that you are able to metabolize your own inner strength and knows that you will naturally grow.
2. Coaches interact with you in a very systematic way to bring forth your strengths and capabilities. They facilitate results by supporting your achievement and development. A Coach is not easy on you and yet despite their demanding nature, coaches are compassionate. A Coach brings forth your best without being harsh or disrespectful. Coaches help you grow and develop and go beyond your fears and doubts.
3. You:
   a) help people become capable and confident.
   b) see their inner strengths, potential and capabilities.
   c) create the environment and stimulation so you can be your best and really shine.
   d) see people as talented and capable.
   e) speak to a person's magnificence and hold a high standard of performance.
   f) motivate people to stretch beyond their normal bounds and do incredible things by believing in them
   g) balance patience with high expectations

RESOLVE
TO BALANCE YOUR STRENGTHS

1. Ensure the person/team understands and is aligned to the goals and tasks.
2. Connect people's tasks to their personal values and company values.
3. Let them know you are absolutely committed to their success.
4. Ask and listen rather than tell.
5. Acknowledge progress when you see it.
6. Be candid.
7. Be enthusiastically and consistently supportive.
8. Capture learnings and best practices and bring them forward.
9. Communicate, communicate, communicate.

The **Cynic** extinguishes any positivity with their negative view of the world and belief that people are inherently bad.

Everybody lies.

The **Mentor** leads people to recognize their patterns and leads them to discover more about themselves and make choices that facilitate their growth, development and evolution over the long term.

Drama   **Leadership**

Vt Victim	Re Resigned	Sp Suspicious	En Envious	Df Defensive	In Inspired	Cr Creative	Cu Curious	Cm Committed	Vi Visionary
Ad Adversary	Bl Blaming	Sr Sarcastic	Ag Angry	Fs Frustrated	Eg Engaged	Pa Passionate	Hu Humorous	Ac Accountable	Av Activator
Rs Rescuer	Su Superior	Cn Controlling	Ha Hidden Agenda	Ar Arrogant	Hm Humble	Tp Transparent	Tr Trusting	Sp Supportive	Co Coach
Cy Cynic	Sk Skeptical	Ct Critical	Is Insulted	Jg Judgmental	Ap Accepting	Cf Confident	Ob Objective	Md Mindful	Mn Mentor

Negative Intention   Choice   Positive Intention
Shadows   Strengths

Notes

. . . .

. . . .

. . . .

. . . .

. . . .

. . . .

. . . .

. . . .

. . . .

. . . .

. . . .

. . . .

Cynic

['si-nik]

1. **showing contempt for human nature and accepted standards of honesty or morality by one's actions, especially by actions that exploit the scruples of others**
2. **distrusting or disparaging the motives of others**
3. **bitterly or sneeringly distrustful or pessimistic; holding a low opinion of humanity**

RECOGNIZE
YOUR THOUGHTS, FEELINGS & ENERGY

1. "Nothing will ever change."
2. "Being optimistic is a complete waste of time."
3. "It's stupid to expect that anything good will come out of this."
4. "You are so naive, don't you see what is going on?"
5. "Just keep your head down and wait it out."
6. "Love is not realistic."

You hose down any hope with what you think is a realistic point of view.

REALIZE
WHAT IS DRIVING YOUR MINDSET

1. You are afraid of disappointment.
2. Cynicism is intellectual cowardice, not intelligence.
3. You are pretending to be too smart to think anything can change.

4. You think you are too smart to get emotionally involved.
5. You don't believe that anything will ever amount to much.
6. You say no to everything automatically.
7. You hose down any positivity with your poisoned outlook.
8. You are deathly afraid of feeling disappointed so you have decided that it's all wrong and all not worth investing any interest or energy.
9. You've traded hope for passive anger.
10. You are not tough. You are playing it safe and avoiding risk by never allowing any new energy or possibility into your life. You are taking the easy way out.
11. Cynics are afraid. You pass judgment on anyone who is trying to make a difference and ridicule the efforts of individuals and organizations that are working hard.
12. What comes out of your mouth is poisonous and attempts to shatter other people's dreams so they can join you in your lifeless misery of dashed hopes.

RESOLVE
▮▮ ▮▮▮▮ ▮▮▮▮▮▮▮

1. Take a moment and a deep breath. Step back and look at what you truly want in your life.
2. Choose to let go of feeling safe.
3. Being cynical seems like the right thing but its protection is a trap.
4. You are not believing anything good can happen for you.
5. Start believing positively in yourself and stop believing the negative things people have told you.
6. Set realistic expectations for yourself. Once you accomplish your goal, thank yourself.
7. Stop being so hard on yourself. The world is not a perfect place.
8. Discover your vision in life and ignite your passion for it.
9. Speak to the positives and what life can be.

Mn

Mentor

[**men**-tawr]

1. an influential senior sponsor or supporter
2. brings forth wisdom and expertise in others
3. has specific knowledge, skills or experience

RECOGNIZE
YOUR THOUGHTS, FEELINGS & ENERGY

1. "What have you learned about how you approach your work from the last three projects you were on?"
2. "How do you think you will evolve and change over the next 5 years?"
3. "I see and feel beneath the surface of things to understand what the deeper nature is."
4. "What is important to me in working with you goes beyond your current position and beyond your career at a specific company."
5. "What are you learning from your pain?"

You honor the people that have come to you as a mentor.

REALIZE
WHAT IS DRIVING YOUR MINDSET

1. You are deeply committed to the development of the person.
2. You sit in a place of looking for patterns of success and patterns that limit.
3. You help a person make the choices that will facilitate their growth.
4. You are focused on developing a person's knowledge and expertise.
5. You do not avoid any situation or pain but rather look for the learning that can come out of it.
6. You see their patterns and ask questions that will lead them to discover more about themselves.
7. You reveal to people how they are thinking and how they can think differently to evolve themselves.
8. You promote their success, not your own.

RESOLVE
TO BALANCE YOUR STRENGTHS

1. Align yourself with their vision and values.
2. Look for how their long-term development (your primary objective) will benefit their current performance.
3. Continually help shift them out of the weeds to a bigger picture of themselves.

CHECK YOUR TUDE ®

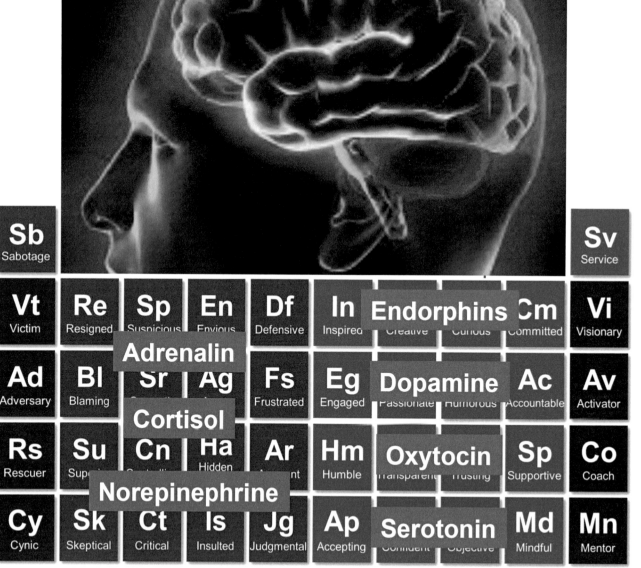

Neuro-Science of Attitude

Sb Sabotage									Sv Service
Vt Victim	Re Resigned	Sp Suspicious	En Envious	Df Defensive	In Inspired	Creative	Curious	Cm Committed	Vi Visionary
Ad Adversary	Bl Blaming	Sr	Ag	Fs Frustrated	Eg Engaged	Passionate	Humorous	Ac Accountable	Av Activator
Rs Rescuer	Su Sup	Cn	Ha Hidden	Ar	Hm Humble	Transparent	Trusting	Sp Supportive	Co Coach
Cy Cynic	Sk Skeptical	Ct Critical	Is Insulted	Jg Judgmental	Ap Accepting	Confident	Objective	Md Mindful	Mn Mentor

Adrenalin

Cortisol

Norepinephrine

Endorphins

Dopamine

Oxytocin

Serotonin

Negative Intention
Shadows

Choice

Positive Intention
Strengths

© 2015 James Peal

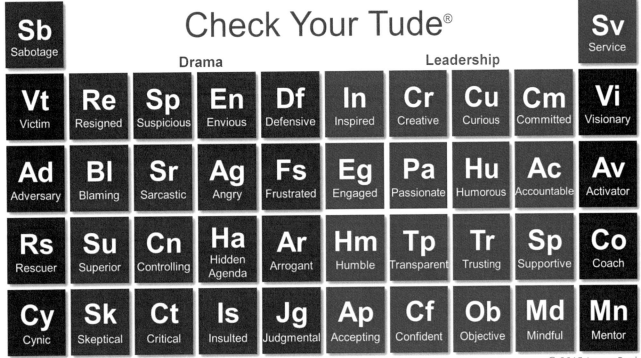

Scan the chart

What are your key strengths?

What are the places where you get tend to get stuck in negativity?

When you are operating from Drama, what is the impact of your attitude on others?

Attitudes in Meetings

What attitudes do you see and play in meetings?

5 Steps to Checking Your Attitude

1. Identify your top 2-3 strengths.

2. What situation/person triggers you to go into a **Negative** attitude?
   - Where do you go?
   - What is the thought or conclusion that starts you spinning in a negative way?

3. Step into **Choice**. Pause for a moment.
   - Take a few deep breaths to calm your thoughts.

4. Identify the **Positive** attitudes that would be useful in that situation.
   - What would be different if you operated from that positive attitude?

5. What reminder/anchor can you use to shift to the Positive attitude(s) in the future?

Check Your Attitude Coaching

The steps to become aware of your negative limiting mindsets and shift to a positive and productive mindset.

1. What are your Positive Intention Strengths?
2. What situation/person triggers you to go into a **Negative Intention Shadow**?
   - Where do you go?
   - What is the thought or conclusion that starts you spinning?
3. Step into **Choice Point**. Pause for a moment.
   - Take a few breaths to clear your emotional palette and calm your thoughts.
4. What Positive Intention Strengths would be useful in this situation?
   - Play the situation in your mind from your Positive Intention Strengths.
   - What difference does it make in how you think, feel and act?
5. What **reminder/anchor** can you put in place to shift yourself quickly to your Positive Intention Strengths next time?

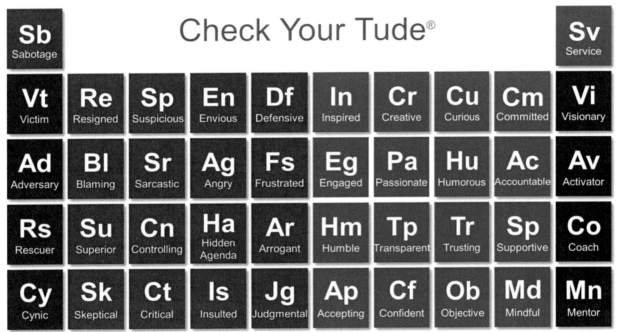

CHECK YOUR TUDE®

Coaching Notes

1. Identify your top 2-3 strengths.

2. What situation/person triggers you to go into a **Negative** attitude?

   • Where do you go?

   • What is the thought or conclusion that starts you spinning in a negative way?

3. Step into **Choice**. Pause for a moment.

   • Take a few deep breaths to calm your thoughts.

4. Identify the **Positive** attitudes that would be useful in that situation.

   • What would be different if you operated from that positive attitude?

5. What reminder/anchor can you use to shift to the Positive attitude(s) in the future?

Notes

. . . .

. . . .

. . . .

. . . .

. . . .

. . . .

. . . .

. . . .

. . . .

. . . .

. . . .

. . . .

Balance your strengths

Balance your Visionary strength of creative new ideas with objective facts and data (Mentor.) Facts and data will

make your vision realistic, connected and more reachable. Incorporate milestones to reach your vision (Activator.) Include the WIIFM (what's in it for me) so that people will see how they will benefit from the vision.

Balance your Activator strength of taking action with concern for people (Coach.) Connecting your plans with

people and their personal experience will make your plans for action motivating, engaging and meaningful. Connect your action plan to the overall direction (Visionary) and the facts and background data that has gone into the decision making.

Balance your Coach strength of caring for people and their performance by linking their actions to concrete goals

& plans and progress metrics (Activator.) Integrate and link your work to the new ideas and benefits of the vision and overall direction (Visionary.) Provide the factual basis and systems of thinking that has gone into the project so they can fully understand the "why" (Mentor.)

Balance your Mentor command of facts & data/wisdom with the creative energy and imagination of the Visionary. Link their long term development with

their current performance as a reality check (Coach.) Establish a strong coherent action plan (Activator) that moves them toward their project goals.

Development Notes

1. Identify your top attitude strength for the key situations you find yourself in at work.

   (You can use the Maximize Strengths Feature on the website: www.checkyourtude.biz to determine the order of your attitude strengths.)

2. For each of your top strengths, how can you balance them with strengths from other rows?

3. Strength   Balance

4. Strength   Balance

5. Strength   Balance

CHECK YOUR TUDE®

Communication & Coaching Strategies

Relationship — Rapport

Rapport

Body Matching — posture, gestures

Face Mirroring — expressions, eyes

Vocal Matching — tone, tempo, volume, emphasis, pauses

Intensity Matching

Speak the Undeniable Truth

Conversation Cycle

INFORM
Self disclose

INVITE
Ask Questions

LISTEN
Give full attention

ACKNOWLEDGE
Repeat essence

5 Degrees of Alignment

5th	Owner
4th	On Board
3rd	Bobble Head
2nd	On a position
1st	Out of the game

Strategies to move out of Sabotage

2 step process — go across and down one row

Victim

Vt Victim	**Victim - get in touch with your vision**	**Vi** Visionary
Ad Adversary	**AND take action toward your vision**	**Av** Activator

Adversary

Ad Adversary	**Adversary - focus on the action steps forward**	**Av** Activator
Rs Rescuer	**AND coach the person for success**	**Co** Coach

Rescuer

Rs Rescuer	**Rescuer - coach people rather than take over**	**Co** Coach
Cy Cynic	**AND mentor for long term growth**	**Mn** Mentor

Cynic

Vt Victim	**AND ignite the fire for your vision**	**Vi** Visionary
Cy Cynic	**Cynic - believe in people and mentor them**	**Mn** Mentor

Strategies to move out of Sabotage

2 step process — go across and down one row

Victim

Vt Victim	**Victim - get in touch with your vision**	**Vi** Visionary
Ad Adversary	**AND take action toward your vision**	**Av** Activator

- What is it you are trying to accomplish?
- If you were successful what would happen?
- What are some options you have not tried yet?
- What is a small step (are steps) you can take toward your goal?
- What do you need to take that step(those steps)?
- When will you take that step(s)?

Adversary

Ad Adversary	**Adversary - focus on the action steps forward**	**Av** Activator
Rs Rescuer	**AND coach the person for success**	**Co** Coach

1. What do you want to happen?
2. What is blocking that taking place?
3. Put yourself in their shoes:
    - What is going on from them?
    - What is their experience of you?
4. What constructive coaching can you provide that will ensure their success?
5. When will you have that conversation?

Strategies to move out of Sabotage

2 step process — go across and down one row

Rescuer

Rs Rescuer	Rescuer - coach people rather than take over	Co Coach
Cy Cynic	AND mentor for long term growth	Mn Mentor

1. What does this person need to know or be able to do to be successful?
2. Rather than doing it yourself, how can you coach them to do it for themselves and own it?
3. When will you do this?
4. How can you plan to pass on what you know to them for the long term?

Cynic

Vt Victim	AND ignite the fire for your vision	Vi Visionary
Cy Cynic	Cynic - believe in people and mentor them	Mn Mentor

1. What are the major changes that need to happen?
2. What would it be like if everything was working the way it should be?
3. How can you support people toward this end?
4. What would happen if you were to motivate people to make everything work?

Check Your Tude

Attitudes Index

Re

Resigned

[ri-**zahynd**]

1. withdraw, abdicate, renounce, quit, leave, give up
2. a submissive unresisting attitude; passive acquiescence
3. the grief you feel when you give up – death of a future

RECOGNIZE
YOUR THOUGHTS, FEELINGS & ENERGY

1. "Why try? It is not going to make any difference."
2. "I really don't care anymore."
3. "It is overwhelming. I can't."
4. "Nothing ever goes right for me."
5. "No one appreciates me."
6. "Life is crap."
7. "If only _____, then I could____." "I can't because _____."

Your energy is depressed & deflated. You feel weighed down. You don't feel like doing anything.

REALIZE
WHAT IS DRIVING YOUR MINDSET

1. The payoff for being resigned is that you never have to make an effort. You can stay in your comfort zone of complaints and despair so that you don't have to take any more risks. It's a way of staying completely safe even despite your complaints to yourself or to the world that you're helpless against the situation and you feel hopeless.
2. You are addicted to the idea that the negative past will be your negative future. You see no hope, no change that is possible.
3. You've given up on any possibility in the future. You are telling yourself you can't because of some external circumstance that you are unwilling to let go of and thereby giving up your experience of choice.
4. You tell yourself that being depressed is better than being disappointed again.
5. It will not be easy getting your energy up to move forward.

RESOLVE
TO MOVE FORWARD

1. How long do you want to be miserable and feel sorry for yourself?
2. To get out of a Victim mindset ask yourself: What do I really want in life? Commit to your vision!
3. Step into the future that you truly want and feel the positive energy of your future.
4. Commit to your life and take action immediately (small steps are fine) toward your goal - go for it, no matter what. Action toward your future is transformational.
5. Notice when you are complaining about how you can't do something because_____. No more excuses. There are other options you just have not explored.
6. Stop complaining about how you feel wronged or undervalued or powerless.
7. Notice where you are thinking, "I have to...." and switch it to, "I choose to..."
8. Where you think, you have to ask, "What if you didn't?"
9. Move forward without proof. That is commitment.
10. Only you can do something for yourself. Even though you may feel like you have no energy, take a small step toward what you want.
11. Help someone else be or feel better.
12. Surround yourself with healthy motivated people.
13. Nourish your body. Eat healthy food, drink lots of water, get sleep, and exercise regularly.

Cm

Committed
[*kuh*-**mit**-ted]

1. to entrust, to give in trust or charge; consign
2. to pledge oneself to a position on an issue or question
3. to bind or obligate, as by pledge or assurance

RECOGNIZE
**YOUR THOUGHTS,
FEELINGS & ENERGY**

1. "I am determined to follow through no matter what."
2. "I will deliver what I said I would, when I said I would."
3. "Nothing will stop me."
4. "You can count on me to follow through."
5. "I have no doubts about him/her delivering as promised."

You are determined. You are mentally and emotionally calm and assured.

REALIZE
**WHAT IS DRIVING
YOUR MINDSET**

1. You are willing to do whatever it takes to get there. You are going to do it no matter what.
2. Tenacious and open, you embrace what's around you, yet you don't give up what you have internally made up your mind about. You are truly being present.
3. You know obstacles will emerge and that you will successfully overcome them as you accomplish your goal.
4. You are free to act fully with your full heart and with your full intention, with all of your skills.
5. Commitment means you go forward when there are gaps in evidence or encouragement to go forward.
6. Commitment is a stretch that takes you out of your comfort zone.

RESOLVE
**TO BALANCE
YOUR STRENGTHS**

1. Create a plan and follow through until it's complete.
2. Focus on the details of getting there. Make sure everyone knows the path forward and how progress will be measured.
3. Support people in their day-to-day tasks.
4. Stay awake and mindful of what is going on around you with people and processes. Respond and focus as things change.
5. Speak your vision freely, engage concerns and questions from those around you. It is normal for people to doubt. Help them see their way forward. Stay the course.
6. Ask people what's in it for them and link their drivers to the vision.
7. Validate, acknowledge and celebrate the small steps forward.

CHECK YOUR TUDE

Sp

Suspicious

[*suh*-**spish**-*uhs*]

1. **tendency to doubt the trustworthiness of appearances and therefore to believe that one has detected possibilities of something unreliable,**

2. **assuming that something is not being revealed that will harm you - wary, leery**

3. **inclined to suspect, especially inclined to suspect evil, dubious**

CHECK YOUR TUDE ®

RECOGNIZE
YOUR THOUGHTS, FEELINGS & ENERGY

1. "I know you are up to something.""You are not saying what you really mean."

2. "I just know you are talking about me behind my back...and making me look bad."

3. "You are just trying to get ahead of me."

4. "I just know they're up to something."

5. "I just know they're trying to take advantage of me."

You are hyper alert and uncomfortable in your skin. You feel exposed and vulnerable on one side and searching for evidence to justify your paranoia that you never can seem to get on the other side.

REALIZE
WHAT IS DRIVING YOUR MINDSET

1. You are afraid because you are expecting some sort of attack or threat. You don't feel powerful.

2. You think they have hidden motives so you don't believe what the other says. You never truly engage or have real conversations with the other person. You don't really talk with them directly.

3. You're out of touch with yourself and therefore cannot adequately or accurately sense other people, which makes you suspicious of everyone.

4. Being suspicious keeps others at a distance and gives you the illusion of safety. You think that your suspicion keeps you from being hurt but really you are just missing out on what life has to offer.

5. Your suspicion of others creates a negative response from others. They feel repelled by you. They can become defensive or just wonder what you are really thinking about them and imagine it is something negative.

6. You are oblivious to how your suspicious mindset is creating others to be uncomfortable and suspicious of you.

RESOLVE
TO MOVE FORWARD

1. Regardless of the other person, identify where you are not experiencing being confident. What are you not feeling confident about? What do you need to do for yourself to restore your confidence?

2. Be curious about the other person. Engage and ask the questions you have on your mind. Ask them about their agenda and intentions. Give them the opportunity to reveal their agenda. Identify your "real" questions, then ask from a place of neutrality.

3. Clarify your relationship with them so that you can move forward

4. Strengthen your relationships where trust exists: Ask yourself, "How can I create this feeling in my other relationships?"

Cu

Curious

[**kyoo** r-ee-*uh* s]

1. arousing or exciting speculation, interest, or attention through being inexplicable or highly unusual; odd; strange
2. eager to learn or know; inquisitive, exploration, investigation and learning, evident by observation in human and many animal species

RECOGNIZE
YOUR THOUGHTS, FEELINGS & ENERGY

1. "I wonder how this works."
2. "How did you do that?"
3. "I didn't notice this before, did you?"
4. "What were the decisions that you made?"
5. "When was this created?"
6. "Who was involved?"
7. "Where were the biggest improvements?"

You lean into topics and situations with discovery questions on your mind. You want to go beyond what appears to be on the surface.

REALIZE
WHAT IS DRIVING YOUR MINDSET

1. You are driven to ask questions and to seek a deeper level of understanding than what appears on the surface.
2. You use the questions what, where, when, how, and who to go from the surface of what is presented to a deeper understanding. Your mind works like a tree and the questions and their answers lead to deeper questions.
3. You are deeply interested and without prompting you naturally want to understand how it all works and/or are taking in all of the nuances.
4. You are moving toward something with delightful questions in your mind.
5. You are delighted by asking questions and wondering how things work.
6. A childlike wonder and marveling at how it all works.

RESOLVE
TO BALANCE YOUR STRENGTHS

1. Invite surprise and delight.
2. Explore new things, a variety of sense, sights, sounds, sensations that you haven't experienced yet.
3. Always explore the edges of what is known. Look for what you don't know.
4. Ask lots of questions from a delightful place of surprise, and people will catch on and begin asking the same types of questions.
5. Once you discover something, communicate it to others. Make the connection of how your discovery adds value and how it can lead to constructive insight or action.
6. Acknowledge your sources; make them valuable contributors to your discovery.

CHECK YOUR TUDE ®

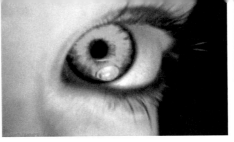

Envious

[**en**-vee-*uhs*]

1. a bitter state or hatred induced by another having something more than oneself

2. goes to incredible lengths to see the envied person experience even an ounce of pain compared to what is their life.

3. wants people to dislike you because they are so jealous.

RECOGNIZE
YOUR THOUGHTS, FEELINGS & ENERGY

1. "He/she doesn't deserve to have that. I should be the one who has that."

2. "What makes her/him think she/he is so special?"

3. "What they have is crap anyway and I don't want it."

4. "They/she/he are privileged, I hate them."

5. "They don't even appreciate what they have."

Things seem unjust and you feel resentful, bitter and angry. Your feelings are convoluted and complicated.

REALIZE
WHAT IS DRIVING YOUR MINDSET

1. You are angry because you realize that you have cheated yourself from the opportunity to "have" something that you want. But rather than face how you have cheated yourself and said no to yourself, you make it someone else's fault and blame them for what they have.

2. You are too busy comparing negatively what you have to what someone else has. You are projecting that someone else is unjustly violating your right to have something that you think you should have.

3. You are telling yourself that you are unworthy or incapable in some way.

4. Not only are you rendered unhappy by envy, but you wish to inflict negativity on others.

5. It's much easier just to sit back and blame other people for their success rather than take full accountability and apply yourself 100 percent to get what it is that you want.

6. Your payoff is that you don't have to get off your butt and do something with your life.

7. There's nothing stopping you except your own self-doubt and self-pity.

RESOLVE
TO MOVE FORWARD

1. Whatever you see in others, you can have for yourself. It won't be handed to you. You need to create it for yourself.

2. Build your self-concept. Start looking inward and identify, acknowledge and fortify your positive qualities.

3. You are equal to other people. No better or worse.

4. Stop being an angry pity-filled bystander. Stop being so self-righteous about how wrong other people are.

5. Get off your butt and focus on what you want to create for your life.

6. Focus on your own inner positive qualities and creativities.

7. Turn your attentions to your own personal goals and forget about what someone else has.

8. Let go of comparing yourself to others in a negative light. Someone will always have more than you and someone would be grateful to have what you have.

9. Learn how to be satisfied with what you have or motivated to work for more.

10. Get inspired about your life and the journey you are on.

Creative

[kree-**ey**-tiv]

1. the ability to transcend and/or bend traditional ideas, rules, conventions, patterns and create meaningful new ideas, forms, methods, etc.
2. characterized by originality of thought; having or showing imagination
3. designed to or tending to stimulate the imagination

RECOGNIZE
YOUR THOUGHTS, FEELINGS & ENERGY

1. "Amazing how many ways you can look at this idea."
2. "If I was starting from scratch, what would this look like?"
3. "What if we had never thought of this idea, what would we come up with?"
4. "OK, we can't use anything we have used before, let's see what we come up with."
5. "Let's look at this idea from the future back to now and see what it looks like."

You are delighted with a blank canvas. You enjoy molding a nothing into something.

REALIZE
WHAT IS DRIVING YOUR MINDSET

1. Novelty and new delight you.
2. You have confidence when your mind is blank. You can wait for ideas to emerge.
3. You have figured out your formula for creativity.
4. You enjoy change for change's sake.
5. You see sounds and hear colors.
6. You are fascinated with the boundaries and edges of things and ideas and how to go beyond those boundaries.
7. You enjoy solving impossible situations.

RESOLVE
TO BALANCE YOUR STRENGTHS

1. Optimize your environment including the place and people. Make it how you want it to be most creative.
2. Give yourself time to incubate your ideas.
3. Get to know your rhythm of creativity – you may need to lock yourself away for days at a time, etc.... Fine-tune yourself.
4. Once your creation has been formed, appreciate it, then if appropriate, describe the context and background that supports it.
5. Mentor and coach others to be creative. Create creative environments for others.
6. When it makes sense, look for how your ideas add value. Your creation is new; where does it take us? What is the "so what" of how your creation adds to what exists?

CHECK YOUR TUDE ®

Defensive

[dih-**fen**-siv]

1. excessively concerned with guarding against the real or imagined threat of criticism,
2. injury to one's ego, or exposure of one's shortcomings
3. made or carried on for the purpose of resisting attack

RECOGNIZE
YOUR THOUGHTS, FEELINGS & ENERGY

1. "It's not my fault."
2. "Yes but..."
3. "You did ____." (accusation)
4. "Yes, but look at what you did." (deflection)
5. "All I did was..." (minimize accountability)

You feel like you have been punched so you want to punch back.

REALIZE
WHAT IS DRIVING YOUR MINDSET

1. You feel that you have been attacked and must fight back with emotion to maintain yourself.
2. You have interpreted what the other person said or did in a negative way and consider your interpretation or their action or words as the truth and not your perception of what is going on.
3. You think you're at fault and you fight back with emotion, not logic.
   a. You stay safe, self-righteous and protected and avoid input or criticism.
   b. You're unwilling to hear anything else - other possibilities.
   c. It's to cover up your self-perceived weakness.
   d. You can't truly appreciate what the other person's intention really was.
4. You think there's something wrong with you and you have to protect it.
5. You think you you've lost, either emotional, standing, pride, money.
6. Your interpretation of what they said or did may have nothing to do with the other person's intention.
7. Your defensiveness/close-mindedness is an attack on their point of view.
8. You are triggering the same defensive response in the other person.

RESOLVE
TO MOVE FORWARD

1. Keep your mouth shut. Take a step back. Take a breath. Take a time-out. Cool down. Let that head of steam dissipate. If you speak when your buttons are pushed you will create a negative reaction in the other person. Don't speak until you are calm.
2. Go look in the mirror and make a funny face at yourself.
3. Put yourself in their shoes – take on their point of view and let them win; you will win too.
4. The more you defend your position the more you get locked into negativity. It's fine to hold your ground, just don't get stuck there.
5. Engage and verify. Hear the other point of view. Ask questions. Find out what's going on over there. Ask them what they meant by what they said or what their intention was behind their actions.
6. What are you defending?
   a. Is there any truth in what they are saying?
   b. What could you learn from the other point of view?
   c. What if they didn't mean what you thought they did?
   d. Replace "yes, but" with "yes, and."
7. Acknowledge the place where you felt attacked or hurt and find some things about yourself that you can truly appreciate. Build your self-esteem.
8. Acknowledge what you are doing right.
9. Ask them what they meant when they said _____.

In

Inspired

[in-**spahy**^{uh}**rd**]

1. **aroused, animated, or imbued with the spirit to do something**
2. **to be filled with an animating energy**
3. **feeling moved by the past, present and/or future**

RECOGNIZE
YOUR THOUGHTS, FEELINGS & ENERGY

1. "I can hardly wait to work on this project!!!"
2. "I feel so much energy all I want to do is smile."
3. "My team goes out of their way to do what it takes; it just feels great to be on this team."
4. "Achieving this will be incredible."
5. "Everyone around me is filled with positive energy."

You feel elevated from the inside out and/or from the outside to move toward some goal or ideal.

REALIZE
WHAT IS DRIVING YOUR MINDSET

1. Your work is aligned with your inner purpose in life. There is a natural flow to your energy and you are in a "good mood" and have lots of energy.
2. Inspiration is physical. Your body is aligned to allow the free flow of energy.
3. You have struck a chord – a natural association of ideas and sudden unison of thought.
4. Is reaching beyond what's apparent into the unknown with a faith and belief.
5. As you're inspired others will very naturally be able to feel that energy within themselves.
6. Inspiration is what happens when our consciousness is lifted; it's the act of lifting up that has us feel inspired.

RESOLVE
TO BALANCE YOUR STRENGTHS

1. Remember your internal source of inspiration. Don't look outside yourself for inspiration.
2. Focus on your commitments.
3. Stay in tune with those around you.
4. Keep your body healthy and tuned so the energy can flow.
5. Do not become a zealot and try to sell others on what inspires you.
6. Inspiration at its best creates inspiration in other people. By being inspired you will become an example for inspiration rather than pushing it on people.

CHECK YOUR TUDE®

Blaming

[bleym-eng]

1. to place the responsibility for a fault, error, what went wrong, etc.; culpability, holding responsible
2. making negative statements about an individual or group that their action or actions are socially or morally irresponsible

RECOGNIZE
YOUR THOUGHTS, FEELINGS & ENERGY

1. "It's your fault."
2. "They are failing.."
3. "They are doing it all wrong."
4. "If they had not screwed up, we would be on time."
5. "They made some huge mistakes that made my team mess up."
6. "It is his fault, we had nothing to do with it."

You immediately accuse others as the responsible party.

REALIZE
WHAT IS DRIVING YOUR MINDSET

1. You're on the attack, tearing somebody else down. You don't see that your blaming is a covert way you excuse yourself from taking responsibility and is a cover for not feeling powerful.

2. You find power in pointing our what's wrong with others and finding who is at fault rather than seeking a solution. You see yourself as the judge and jury that need no further evidence. "Guilty as charged" is your motto.

3. Your self-righteous attack stance sets others up to respond to you defensively. You will interpret their reaction to you as evidence you are right about their guilt. If you feel that someone is blaming you it is still the mindset of blame – just the other side of the coin.

4. You are resisting looking at yourself and your imperfections. You never do any introspection or take a view of yourself that there is room for improvement.

5. You let yourself off the hook by avoiding being accountable.

RESOLVE
TO MOVE FORWARD

1. Hold yourself accountable for everything FIRST.

2. Be the role model for accountability. If you hold yourself accountable others will follow your lead. By holding yourself accountable you create safety for others to work.

3. Rather than point out what is wrong ask yourself, "What can I say or do to make others successful?"

4. Approach as a coach who is committed to the others' success.

5. People learn more and feel better when they are shown how to do something rather than being told how they were wrong.

6. Begin the discussion by asking the person(s) about their perception of the situation and work towards a solution from where they are.

Ac

Accountable

[*uh*-koun-*tuh*-**bul**]

1. the person or entity that others can count on to deliver on their promises
2. has the final decision-making authority
3. responsible to someone or for some action; answerable
4. you can trust

RECOGNIZE
YOUR THOUGHTS, FEELINGS & ENERGY

1. "I am the one leading that project and responsible for the results."
2. "You can count on me to deliver as promised."
3. "I will be there exactly at 10:00 a.m."
4. "You can ask the other customers about the service they received from our team."
5. "We have a 10-year history of delivering under budget."

You feel confident, open and ready to take decisive action.

REALIZE
WHAT IS DRIVING YOUR MINDSET

1. Being accountable forces you out of your comfort zone, keeps you on your toes, gives you freedom to creatively solve problems and create results.
2. Accountable is one of the foundations for trust and integrity.
3. You must remain vigilant from inception to completion.
4. Often you must reach beyond your normal boundaries to ensure success.
   • "I own the process from end to end."
5. There is a tension, a risk involved in being accountable because if things go wrong people will look to you. "The buck stops with me."

RESOLVE
TO BALANCE YOUR STRENGTHS

1. Stay execution oriented.
2. Only make promises that you can keep.
3. Communicate immediately if things start to go off track. Let stakeholders know what is happening and establish a plan to address the problems that have arisen.
4. Enhance your engagement of others in the goals.
5. When you hold someone accountable ensure they are clear on the deliverables, are capable, and have the resources to deliver. Support their success by having consistent communication with them. Let them know your job is to make them successful.
6. As a leader take the hit for your team when things go wrong. You have their back. Never throw someone under the bus.
7. When they go right, celebrate their success.

CHECK YOUR TUDE ®

Sarcastic

[sahr-**kas**-tik]

1. Ridicule, biting, sneering, ironical taunt, mockery or making cutting jibes used harshly, often crudely and contemptuously, for destructive purposes
2. A sharp remark usually conveyed through understatement
3. Is present in the spoken word and manifested chiefly by vocal intonation

CHECK YOUR TUDE ®

RECOGNIZE
YOUR THOUGHTS, FEELINGS & ENERGY

1. "Really?"
2. "There are no stupid questions, just stupid people."
3. "I can explain it to you, I can't understand it for you."
4. "Where did you learn how to dress like that?"
5. "What's the matter, can't you take a joke?"
6. "He's not the sharpest knife in the drawer."

You are disgusted and hold yourself and others in contempt. Your humor is based on tearing someone down.

REALIZE
WHAT IS DRIVING YOUR MINDSET

1. You are judging that person inferior and insisting on making fun of them in a derogatory way.
2. You feel righteous and justified in your hostility because you think that you have "tried" to make things work in the past and they just didn't listen.
3. You stopped caring about yourself and want to take it out on someone to make them look bad.
4. You are afraid of just stating what you are angry about out of fear of being fired or ostracized.
5. You're constantly lashing out pretending to be funny, but your humor is at someone's expense.
6. You are in a very caustic loathing, fearful place.
7. You don't realize that your cocky self-righteous sarcasm is inflicting deep pain in others and poisoning your own outlook on life.

RESOLVE
TO MOVE FORWARD

1. Step into the other person's shoes and feel the harshness of your sarcastic comments. Do you really want to inflict pain in others?
2. See others as your equal and look for how you can say what is on your mind and be direct and kind at the same time.
3. Admit that you avoid looking at yourself and owning your imperfections and having compassion for yourself.
4. Appreciate that you are a work in progress and have talents and strengths and places where you are not being all that you can be.
5. Learn how to use self-deprecating humor instead of sarcasm. Practice being humble – part of the greater good.

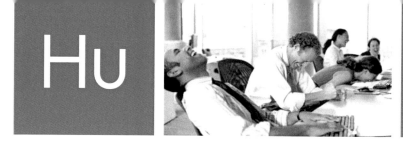

Hu

Humorous

[**hyoo**-mer-*uhs*]

1. creates laughter: an expression of mirth with an audible, vocal expulsion of air from the lungs from a loud burst of sound to a series of quiet chuckles
2. quickness to perceive the amusing, striking, or unusual and to express it cleverly and entertainingly, providing fun; causing amusement

RECOGNIZE
YOUR THOUGHTS, FEELINGS & ENERGY

1. "That was too funny."
2. "I haven't laughed that hard in a long time."
3. "Everybody was thinking it, but he said it."
4. "My belly hurts from laughing."
5. "That was a little twisted but very funny."

You are buoyant and present. You find yourself amused at what is seeming mundane.

REALIZE
WHAT IS DRIVING YOUR MINDSET

1. You win by naturally finding humor in a situation.
2. Humor is reason gone mad.
3. You have a deep appreciation for the irony in life or a situation and can verbalize irony.
4. You are able to spontaneously verbalize your perception of reality in a way that amuses you.
5. You have a combination of surprise and creativity that creates energy flow and lightness.
6. You see a unique perspective and communicate lightheartedly to bring and shift awareness to others.

RESOLVE
TO BALANCE YOUR STRENGTHS

1. Humor is not for everyone. It is for those who want to have fun, enjoy life and feel alive. Invite people to humor rather than force it on them.
2. Stay present – humor happens in the moment.
3. Don't try to be funny – there's nothing worse than somebody who is trying to be funny.
4. Look at the big picture and the finished product which will put this moment into perspective.
5. Create the journey of achieving goals a fun one.
6. Turn sarcasm into self-deprecating humor.

Ag

Angry

[ang-gree]

1. a feeling of great annoyance or antagonism as the result of some real or supposed grievance
2. a strong feeling of displeasure and belligerence aroused by a wrong, or injury
3. the emotion of instant displeasure on account of something evil that presents itself

RECOGNIZE
YOUR THOUGHTS, FEELINGS & ENERGY

1. "I'm shocked that you said/did that."
2. "I'm outraged!"
3. "I'm so pissed off right now!"
4. "You are irritating me no end!"
5. "I want to wring your neck."
6. "Who do you think you are?"

Your adrenaline is flowing and you are ready for a fight. You are seeking an object or person to lash out at and dissipate the bottled up energy you feel.

REALIZE
WHAT IS DRIVING YOUR MINDSET

1. An angry mindset is a defense against pain. What is the pain/anguish/failure that you are avoiding feeling underneath your anger?
2. Your feeling of energy and power is dependent on others feeling bad. You are sure you are right and the other(s) is wrong.
3. You use anger to push people away. You are afraid of feeling helpless, even hurt.
4. You are just being stubborn and close-minded because you are not getting your way and want to make them wrong for not listening to you or doing exactly what you say.
5. Momentary anger alerts us to something that appears wrong or unjust. The Anger mindset is about being right.
6. Anger is punishing yourself.

RESOLVE
TO MOVE FORWARD

1. Keep your mouth shut for a moment.
2. Take a few deep breaths to calm yourself down and tune in.
3. Pause. Stay with your feeling long enough to notice what is really bothering you underneath the surface. It is not what you think you are angry about and not about the other person. If you can pause and breathe into that deeper feeling you will start to feel at peace.
4. What will you feel on a deep level if you don't react with anger?
5. What outcome will benefit both of you?
6. Get over being righteous. No one is that important to hold a grudge forever.
7. Apologize for attacking the other person.
8. Explain your anger instead of expressing it, and you will find solutions instead of arguments.

Passionate

[**pash**-*uh*-nit]

1. an intense emotion compelling feeling, enthusiasm or desire for something
2. intense, driving or overmastering feeling or conviction
3. a feeling of unusual excitement, enthusiasm or compelling emotion

RECOGNIZE
YOUR THOUGHTS, FEELINGS & ENERGY

1. "I feel a strong energy toward what I am doing."
2. "I will deliver what I said I would, when I said I would."
3. "Nothing will stop me."
4. "I want to go beyond what I thought was possible."
5. "Yes!!!"

Your feet are on the ground and you are feeling strong, powerful and exhilarated. Your mind is clearly focused on your goal.

REALIZE
WHAT IS DRIVING YOUR MINDSET

1. You are internally aligned to your greater purpose and values and are confidently taking action toward achieving your goals.
2. You are committed and making tangible progress.
3. You are organically connected to what you are doing.
4. People around you feel your energy and want to join with you. You welcome their participation.
5. You are accepting of life's obstacles and see them as a natural part of making progress.
6. You bring a sense of urgency to the work you are doing but are not pushy or demanding.

RESOLVE
TO BALANCE YOUR STRENGTHS

1. Focus on what you enjoy and direct your energy toward accomplishment.
2. Stay centered.
3. Look for how you can benefit others.
4. Make sure you have cycles of rest to stay in balance.
5. Connect with people around you and coach them toward their goals. Be curious about what makes them tick. Help them get in touch with their values and their purpose in life.
6. Keep moving toward your goals.
7. Bring others along by being passionate and not trying to sell them.
8. Acknowledge and celebrate others' success.

CHECK YOUR TUDE

Fs

Frustrated
[**fruhs**-trey-tid]

1. is the anger that you feel when things are not moving in the direction that you want
2. irritated with the feeling of being powerless in this situation
3. it arises from the perceived resistance to the fulfillment of individual will
4. to make (plans, efforts, etc.) worthless or of no avail

RECOGNIZE
YOUR THOUGHTS, FEELINGS & ENERGY

1. "How many times do I have to go over this?"
2. "Why can't they just do it right?"
3. "Jeeze, this is killing me, it is going so slow!"
4. "If I have to explain this one more time..."
5. "This jerk is soooo stubborn, I can't believe it."

Your energy is high but it is turning back on itself because reality is not moving fast enough. You just want to push through the resistance.

REALIZE
WHAT IS DRIVING YOUR MINDSET

1. You have gone from urgency to impatience.
2. You are unwilling to accept the situation and work with it.
3. You are making the other person wrong for not going the way you want and/or as fast as you want.
4. You are experiencing resistance because you are using force.
5. You are throwing a temper tantrum because things aren't going exactly your way. You're fixed on a single way of doing things.
6. You are insisting on how wrong others are and dramatizing your "heroic" efforts.
7. You think you are justified at being upset with the other person.
8. You are creating a situation where the other person or the situation has to change in order for you to feel satisfied. Even if the change will not satisfy you.

RESOLVE
TO MOVE FORWARD

1. Realize that your impatience is stopping the progress.
2. Take a step back, shift into neutral, stop pushing.
3. Ask: What do I need to learn from this situation? What am I missing? What new way can I approach this problem?
4. Engage and get creative; look at multiple ways of accomplishing the goal.
5. Step into their shoes and find out what is stopping them and help them to be more successful.
6. Find how you can create urgency instead of impatience.
7. Look for ways around the obstacle versus insisting that the obstacle change.

Eg

Engaged

[en-**geyjd**]

1. to occupy the attention or effort
2. to attract and hold fast
3. busy or occupied; involved
4. to bind, as by pledge, promise, contract, or oath

RECOGNIZE
YOUR THOUGHTS, FEELINGS & ENERGY

1. "It is amazing all that it takes to make this happen."
2. "Whew, that was a long and very good day."
3. "All our milestones have been accomplished. We are right on track."
4. "What do you need to succeed at your task?"
5. "OK, let's keep our eyes and ears open during this next phase."

You feel that you are making positive progress. You have your wits about you because this venture requires all of your talents. You feel confident and in control of things.

REALIZE
WHAT IS DRIVING YOUR MINDSET

1. Your energy channeled into a constructive framework..
2. You are creating a positive outcome.
3. You're grasping a hold of things in a constructive way and all of your energy is moving the action forward.
4. You expect and embrace conflict as normal.
5. You bring an urgency to things but are not pushy.
6. You not are only going with the flow, you are creating the flow. You expect the waves, currents and obstacles that come your way and work with and around them.

RESOLVE
TO BALANCE YOUR STRENGTHS

1. Be practical and pragmatic.
2. Listen to others and keep your focus.
3. Link a person's core values to the task or goals so they can see and feel connected personally to their work.
4. Let people know how their job contributes to the success of the whole organization and the goal they are working on.
5. Err on the side of over communication.
6. Pay attention to non-verbal signals that people may be sending you that they have checked out.
7. Consistently ask people what they need to be successful and coach them.
8. Help people prioritize their work when new urgencies arise.
9. Acknowledge people's successes and accomplishments.

CHECK YOUR TUDE

Su

Superior

[sÚ-'pir-ē-ər]

1. **showing a consciousness or feeling of being better than or above others**

2. **covertly or overtly letting people know they are beneath you**

3. **haughty, above-it-all airs**

RECOGNIZE
YOUR THOUGHTS, FEELINGS & ENERGY

1. "I am simply better than you are."

2. "I have more knowledge, experience, skills...."

3. "I suppose you are doing the best you can."

4. "You have to take into account what your starting point was."

5. "I don't have to take you seriously or into consideration."

You feel above others as if it is a fact. Keeping a distance feels comfortable for you.

REALIZE
WHAT IS DRIVING YOUR MINDSET

1. You are a know-it-all.

2. You use knowledge, power, position, experience to position yourself as being above and better than others.

3. You are in constant competition with others, always trying to outdo them. One-upsmanship is draining you and those around you.

4. You surround yourself with people whom you deem inferior to maintain your superiority.

5. You ignore and minimize positive qualities in others.

6. You disengage because you think you are more important than others.

7. You keep people from getting too close for fear they might see through your veneer.

RESOLVE
TO MOVE FORWARD

1. Step out of your role and become a normal person. Get to know the people you work with on a personal level and let them get to know about you personally.

2. While it seems paradoxical to give your position of power away, giving it away is the only way to reach humbleness.

3. Authentically verbally acknowledge people around you for what they bring to work/relationship.

4. Ask yourself, "What can I learn from this person?"

5. Be a source – freely give away all your secrets for success, spread your knowledge – pride yourself on mentoring others.

6. Establish a reputation for how you support and empower success for those who work with you.

CHECK YOUR TUDE ®

Sp

Supportive

[*suh*-**pawr**-tiv]

1. to serve as a foundation for
2. to sustain or withstand without giving way
3. to undergo or endure, especially with patience or submission; tolerate
4. to sustain (a person, the mind, spirits, courage, etc.) under trial or affliction

RECOGNIZE
YOUR THOUGHTS, FEELINGS & ENERGY

1. "How can I help you be successful?"
2. "What do you need right now?"
3. "If I could change one thing to be more effective in working with you, what would that be?"
4. "Let me know how much direction would be useful for you."
5. "I only want to do what is useful for you."

You feel open and willing to be there for the other person by encouraging.

REALIZE
WHAT IS DRIVING YOUR MINDSET

1. You selflessly wish for the other's success.
2. You are there to promote another's greatness.
3. You don't expect anything in return.
4. You believe in other people and see their value despite what they think are their flaws.

RESOLVE
TO BALANCE YOUR STRENGTHS

1. Remind people of how great they are. Validate them. Let them know specifically what they are doing that makes a difference.
2. Let them see how they fit into the big picture and how their work contributes to the overall goals.
3. Be a good teammate. Help others accomplish their goals – do it without expectation for acknowledgment.
4. Encourage people when you see they want to take a risk and are afraid. Let them know the strength you see inside of them and how that makes you feel.
5. Tell someone how thankful you are that they are in your life.

CHECK YOUR TUDE ®

Cn

Controlling

[*kuhn*-**trohl**-ng]

1. **to exercise restraint or direction over; dominate; command**
2. **to hold in check; curb**
3. **to eliminate or prevent the flourishing or spread of**

RECOGNIZE
YOUR THOUGHTS, FEELINGS & ENERGY

1. "Do it my way, otherwise you'll waste time and money."
2. "Obviously I know the right way to do this."
3. "Run your plan by me before taking action."
4. "We have tried that before and it won't work."
5. "Save your good ideas for another project."

You are unsettled by what and how someone might do things.

REALIZE
WHAT IS DRIVING YOUR MINDSET

1. You don't trust that someone can do it better or as good as you can.
2. You are convinced that you know the best way to do something.
3. You excuse your taking over by telling yourself that you don't have time to teach the person.
4. You consistently devalue others' abilities and inflate yours.
5. You think you are indispensable – the world/project will fall apart without you and you want to keep it that way.
6. You are blind to how you are extinguishing creativity and innovation.
7. You are afraid that someone will outshine you.
8. You think you will be left behind.

RESOLVE
TO MOVE FORWARD

1. Acknowledge each person's strengths and emphasize your confidence in them.
2. Think about how you can empower them with your knowledge and abilities.
3. Teach them how to think/view/operate rather than take over.
4. Create risks for others to take where they can be successful.
5. Face your fear of being insignificant; acknowledge value you bring to others.
6. Commit to make the others truly successful in what they do.
7. Take a breath and let go for a minute; realize that you are not losing anything.
8. Let them shine. Lead from behind.

Trusting
[**truhs**-ting]

1. reliance on the integrity, strength, ability, surety, etc., of a person or thing; confidence
2. confident expectation of something; hope
3. a person on whom or a thing on which one relies

RECOGNIZE
YOUR THOUGHTS, FEELINGS & ENERGY

1. "I am safe. Everything is OK."
2. "This is perfect!"
3. "I feel so at home."
4. "I am open."
5. "I am here for you."
6. "I love the people I work with."

You feel at home and at peace. You are open mentally and emotionally without defenses. You intentionally allow another/others to impact you.

REALIZE
WHAT IS DRIVING YOUR MINDSET

1. You are willing to be open and connect authentically with people.
2. You are calm knowing that you can address whatever comes up.
3. You are willing to let go of protecting yourself and you allow others to impact you. In a way you are undefended. When trust is up your guard is down. "You won't harm me."
4. You can see where people have theirs walls up but you do not put yours up
5. Your heart, mind and spirit are open to receiving and you have nothing to gain and nothing to lose.

RESOLVE
TO BALANCE YOUR STRENGTHS

1. Be transparent and authentic.
2. Speak the truth.
3. Do what you say you will.
4. Do not exaggerate, be a straight shooter and people will immediately sense that you're trustworthy.
5. As you move into action, stay connected with your inner self and others.
6. Create and hold clear goals and boundaries and keep them.
7. Hold to your own truth when surrounded by untrustworthiness.

Ha

Hidden Agenda

[**hid**-n] [*uh*-**jen**-d*uh*]

1. an often duplicitously undisclosed plan or motive
2. a wish (and plan) to implement a particular idea without telling anybody even though people will be affected in a negative way

RECOGNIZE
YOUR THOUGHTS, FEELINGS & ENERGY

1. "I will just work around you and you will never know."
2. "Let me tell you some gossip about _____."
3. "If you knew what I was up to, you would be angry."
4. "You are an idiot but I will never tell you."
5. "I will take this up with your boss behind your back."
6. "I will tell you what you want to hear but not the truth."

You feel powerless to be direct. Your power is in being sneaky and covert.

REALIZE
WHAT IS DRIVING YOUR MINDSET

1. You avoid conflict , afraid you will lose the argument; you sneak around trying to get an edge up on others.
2. Either way you feel like the under-dog and that you have to sneak around or that someone has an edge on you that they are keeping secret.
3. You are certain someone is taking advantage of you.
4. You don't believe you can make it by being open and honest.
5. You are not taking full responsibility for your life.
6. You're devaluing yourself because you don't want to risk rejection or ridicule.

RESOLVE
TO MOVE FORWARD

1. Do not hide. Reveal your goals/plan/agenda in an open and honest way and ask for support from others toward your goals.
2. Establish a deeper level of confidence so that you can speak what you want clearly and directly.
3. Be willing to engage and resolve conflict rather than hide out.
4. Let go of secrets.
5. Talk to people. Ask people about their agenda, intentions and outcomes from a place of curiosity rather than suspicion.

Tp

Transparent

[trans-**pair**-*uh*nt]

1. **having the interior immediately accessible**
2. **to afford access**
3. **giving people access to your thinking, feeling and decision-making processes**
4. **letting your intentions be known**

RECOGNIZE
YOUR THOUGHTS, FEELINGS & ENERGY

1. "Here is what I am doing and why I am doing it."
2. "Let me explain how I made the decision."
3. "I would like to understand your thinking and welcome your questions."
4. "Here is what concerns me..."
5. "I often struggle with..."

You feel relaxed and willing to talk about yourself, what makes you tick at work and personally. You invite candid questions about your thinking and decision making and you ask candid questions.

REALIZE
WHAT IS DRIVING YOUR MINDSET

1. You are feeling great courage and openness. You speak your mind so people can see what you're thinking, what you're feeling and what makes you tick.
2. It's not having any corners or edges, or places where you're unwilling to reveal yourself. This does not mean that you reveal everything, sometimes it is not appropriate to do so, but your willingness keeps you open.
3. You don't share every thought or feeling that you are having – you're not hiding anything that is relevant to the topic at hand.
4. When something needs to be held in confidence you let people know, "I am not at liberty to share that information at this time."
5. When making decisions you communicate how you're considering each of the inputs.

RESOLVE
TO BALANCE YOUR STRENGTHS

1. Speak from the heart.
2. Welcome questions about your thought process and decision making.
3. Explain your process without being defensive.
4. Welcome conflict as an opportunity for everyone to learn.
5. Always seek positive intention, especially when it is tough.
6. Be willing to talk about anything and choose what you reveal.
7. Put yourself in the other's shoes and ask yourself, "What are the questions they are thinking?"

CHECK YOUR TUDE ®

Ar

Arrogant

[ar-*uh*-gu*h*nt]

1. overbearing, unwarranted or exaggerated importance, worth or stature
2. foolishly believing that everyone is inferior to you, looks up to you, and should bow down to your graces; a false sense of pride
3. blatantly and disdainfully proud

RECOGNIZE
YOUR THOUGHTS, FEELINGS & ENERGY

1. "I wish you were as good as me... wait, no, I don't wish that at all. Besides, you would never make it."
2. "If only you knew how much better I am than you are."
3. "You have done nothing compared to me."
4. "If only you knew a quarter of what I know."
5. "Your life is not as important as mine."

You are bloated with your self image and are compelled to put everyone down who is around you. You think you are special and should be treated that way.

REALIZE
WHAT IS DRIVING YOUR MINDSET

1. You think that you are better than everyone else and are smug about it. You think you are great, everyone else thinks you are an asshole.
2. You puff yourself up, make yourself feel bigger, self-righteous and justified at the cost of belittling others.
3. Even if you are better than everyone else, your arrogant attitude diminishes your overall value.
4. You don't see other people's importance or contributions and you're blind to how much you hurt them.
5. You're exaggerating your self-importance because you're insecure. You're afraid of not being important.

RESOLVE
TO MOVE FORWARD

1. Get over yourself. Stop trying to impress people with how important you are.
2. It's not about you. Valuing others is more important than blowing your own horn.
3. Verbally acknowledge others. Identify the value that others bring.
4. Rather than focus on what people can do for you, focus on how you can care for them.
5. Whoever comes into your awareness, make them feel valuable.
6. Develop humbleness. See yourself as part of the greater good, rather than the only thing that is good.

Hm

Humble
[huhm-buhl]

1. courteously respectful
2. near the ground, not high or lofty;
   not pretentious or magnificent; unpretending; unassuming
3. not proud or arrogant; modest

RECOGNIZE
YOUR THOUGHTS, FEELINGS & ENERGY

1. "I see you as a beautiful human being."
2. "I will deliver what I said I would, when I said I would."
3. "Nothing will stop me."
4. "You can count on me to follow through."
5. "His/her reputation is sterling."

You are determined. You are mentally and emotionally calm and assured.

REALIZE
WHAT IS DRIVING YOUR MINDSET

1. You see yourself as a small part of the greater good that exists in the world. "I'm a small part of the greatness that is – I accept my place in the universe."
2. You know there is nothing to prove.
3. You are open, vulnerable, no agenda, authentic.
4. You're not comparing yourself to anything.
5. You see the greatness around you and appreciate it from a pure place within you.
6. You can be direct without being harsh because of your total respect for the other person.

RESOLVE
TO BALANCE YOUR STRENGTHS

1. Keep your vision and purpose in life in focus and keep taking positive action to serve others through your purpose in life.
2. When encountering arrogance, smile.
3. Honor and respect others first, then yourself.
4. Be clear about what you want to accomplish and let others know and invite their participation.
5. Stay fully engaged with your goals and aligned with your values.

CHECK YOUR TUDE ®

Sk

Skeptical

[**skep**-tikal]

1. maintains a doubting attitude, as toward values, plans, statements, or the character of others
2. a person who questions the validity or authenticity of something purporting to be factual

RECOGNIZE
YOUR THOUGHTS, FEELINGS & ENERGY

1. "I just don't believe this."
2. "No one could be that good. They must be wanting something."
3. "It may look good but there is no proof to back it up."
4. "They could not have thought this up so quickly."
5. "Prove it to me."

You question everything automatically; you accept nothing at face value and always doubt the integrity of those around you. You experience mental tension trying to figure out the "catch" in what is being presented.

REALIZE
WHAT IS DRIVING YOUR MINDSET

1. It doesn't matter what is said here, you won't believe it because you are too afraid of being vulnerable.

2. You are allergic to imagination and creativity.
3. You are ridged, mechanical, self-righteous and stuck.
4. Nothing will help here because you are too terrified to soften up.
5. Maybe you could just let someone love you completely but more than likely you will make them prove that they love you and they will go away, thus making you right about doubting their love.
6. You have confused a skeptical mindset with mental rigor. We need mental rigor but you are stuck in a "prove it to me" and can't shut it off.
7. I doubt you will get any help here, Click another tile.

RESOLVE
TO MOVE FORWARD

1. Don't confuse a skeptical mindset with mental rigor. We need mental rigor when dealing with work but you are stuck in a "prove it to me"

and can't shut it off and this attitude is leaking over to the personal side of relationships at work and at home.

2. Draw a clear line for your skepticism. Put it to work where it is useful and intentionally shut it off.
3. Nothing will help here if you are too terrified to open your mind and take a risk. Are you too afraid that you will be taken advantage of at work and more than likely at home as well. Check and see if you can open your mind.
4. You may even have doubts about those who are closest to you. Are you trying to make them prove it to you as well. Maybe you could just let someone love you completely but more than likely you will make them prove that they love you and they will go away, thus making you right about doubting even their love.
5. Learn how to laugh at yourself.
6. If you think this is all BS, I doubt you will get any help here, Click another tile.

Md

Mindful
[**mahynd**-*fuh*l]

1. attentive, aware, or careful
2. introspective meditation, self aware
3. able to see the patterns of the mind and not be of them
4. desiring to understand the nature of experience, conscious reality

RECOGNIZE
**YOUR THOUGHTS,
FEELINGS & ENERGY**

1. "Let's step back for a moment and look at how we are approaching this."
2. "I see a recurring pattern in the types of solutions you have been implementing."
3. "What is the difference between how you are thinking about this situation and how you feel about it?"
4. "What are the 3 key things you pay attention to when talking with and listening to someone?"
5. "What are the similarities and differences between the last 3 projects you have worked on?"

You are calmly detached but attentive to what is going on around you.

REALIZE
**WHAT IS DRIVING
YOUR MINDSET**

1. You always see and seek a bigger picture. You see the past, present and future from a neutral vantage point.
2. You do not identify with your thoughts but more noticing the patterns of thinking.
3. You are aware of the interplay between different elements, whether they are inter-psychic or intra-psychic.
4. You see the developmental pathways for the people you work with.
5. You see the causal relationship between perception and emotion and see how people's mental, communication and emotional patterns link together.
6. You to listen deeply and hear what is said and what is not said.
7. You naturally pause before you speak and carefully consider what you say.

RESOLVE
**TO BALANCE
YOUR STRENGTHS**

1. Take time to still your mind every day.
2. Pause and check in to ensure you are in balance.
3. Notice when your emotions are activated and the thoughts that are stimulating your emotions.
4. Take your time to get to know the people you are working with to understand their values, personality features and communication patterns.
5. Assist people to step back from themselves and to become more aware of themselves and their automatic reactions to people and situations.
6. Mindful does not mean actionless. Keep focused on your goals and making forward motion AND be aware.

CHECK YOUR TUDE ®

Ct

Critical

[**krit**-i-k*uhl*]

1. inclined, occupied to find fault or to judge with severity, often too readily
2. verbal or non-verbal personal attack likely to make the individual feel rejected, not accepted or liked, unfairly treated, degraded, dishonored or humiliated
3. can be toward self, others or situation

RECOGNIZE
YOUR THOUGHTS, FEELINGS & ENERGY

1. "Everything about this is wrong."
2. "I'm irritated about how much is wrong here."
3. "You don't know how not to make mistakes."
4. "No matter what I do, nothing I do is right."
5. "There is something wrong with me."

You are irritated about mistakes that are being made and on the attack.

REALIZE
WHAT IS DRIVING YOUR MINDSET

1. You sit in a self-righteous, negative place where you tear things apart, item by item.
2. Even if you are right there is no way for someone to accept your point of view without feeling put down.
3. You're angry about how imperfect you think you are. This erodes your self-confidence and any appreciation you might have for yourself – it's a poison. You treat others the same way.
4. You always set unachievable standards to maintain a negative attitude about not achieving them.
5. You "YES BUT" everything and minimize and/or invalidate the positive.
6. A critical mindset here is not critical thinking. Critical thinking is in the domain of rigor. A critical mindset is mental anger that is not productive.

RESOLVE
TO MOVE FORWARD

1. Realize that everything can be improved, so tearing it apart will not make it better.
2. See where improvements can be made and see it as simply a characteristic, not a negative flaw that deserves condemnation.
3. Ask yourself where your vision of perfection comes from. Where did you learn to be critical? How do you know that something is not perfect – compared to what? How many things in this world are perfect?
4. Take a moment and a deep breath and appreciate yourself. Allow the feeling of wholeness to return. Stop being so hard on yourself. The world is perfectly not a perfect place.
5. Remind yourself daily that you are a work in progress; enjoy the journey.
6. Set realistic expectations for yourself. Once you accomplish your goal, thank yourself.
7. Find 3 things a day to appreciate about yourself.

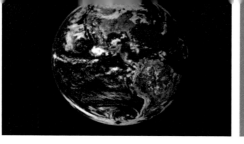

Objective

[*uhb*-**jek**-tiv]

1. not influenced by personal feelings, interpretations or prejudice
2. based on facts; unbiased;
   existing independent of thought or an observer
3. intent upon or dealing with things external to the mind

RECOGNIZE
**YOUR THOUGHTS,
FEELINGS & ENERGY**

1. "Let's step back and get a broader view."
2. "What is another way to look at this?"
3. "What do we know as fact?" "What is your personal opinion?"
4. "Let's find out what _____ thinks about the situation."
5. "Here is what I see. What do you see?"

You are feeling calm and neutral, neither moving toward nor away from any viewpoint or perspective. You are aware of many distinctions but are not compelled toward any of them.

REALIZE
**WHAT IS DRIVING
YOUR MINDSET**

1. Driven to rise above and see multiple perspectives simultaneously without attachment to a specific outcome.
2. Giving equal weight to all choices.
3. Looking at things factually as they are without bias and without judgment.
4. Stepping out of your self-perception and assuming a perspective that is neutral.
5. Neutral emotional quality is present, not emotionally inclined in any particular direction or drawn into any type of emotion.
6. Is able to verbalize what is observed so that others can appreciate your vantage point.

RESOLVE
**TO BALANCE
YOUR STRENGTHS**

1. Distinguish between the facts and your personal feelings about them or the situation. Verbally acknowledge and/or write our your personal biases.
2. It is fine and normal to have a personal perspective attached to feelings; what gives you the strength is your ability to identify them and shift your focus to the facts.
3. Notice when others may be biased by their emotional or ego attachments. Ask questions to clarify their position.
4. Take 3 deep breaths to neutralize your internal feeling responses and then look again. Check to ensure you are emotionally neutral.
5. Change your posture in some way to mark out moving to a neutral frame of mind; e.g., stand up, sit back, move your chair.
6. Be curious about how others are perceiving the situation. Value multiple perspectives in determining an objectivity.

CHECK YOUR TUDE ®

Insulted

[in-**suhlt**-ed]

1. an expression, statement (or sometimes behavior) which is considered degrading, offensive and impolite
2. to attack, assault, offend or demean
3. an insolent or contemptuously rude action or remark; affront

RECOGNIZE
YOUR THOUGHTS, FEELINGS & ENERGY

1. "Who do you think you are?"
2. "You are such an idiot."
3. "You expect me to work here?"
4. "That's not my job." "I don't get paid to do that task."
5. "He's not the sharpest knife in the drawer."

You are offended by what was said or what was put in front of you. You hold others in contempt.

REALIZE
WHAT IS DRIVING YOUR MINDSET

1. Insults are in the ear of the beholder.
2. Being insulted tells you about how you really think about yourself.

3. You think you are above what is being told to you but part of you already gave agreement to it.
4. You are giving agreement to the negative comment the person said about you, then rejecting it and blaming them.
5. Your arrogance closes you off from receiving any new information about yourself, and you are defensive rather than willing to listen and possibly grow.
6. You think you are better than others.

RESOLVE
TO MOVE FORWARD

1. Notice that you are giving power to that person's opinion of you on some level you agreed with what that person said. Otherwise you would not have felt it that way.

2. Where are you giving agreement to what was said? What does that mean about your view of yourself? How can you own your own opinion of yourself? How can you grow, change, develop your self-image to be more self-confident?
3. Ask the person specifically what they meant by that comment to see if they were speaking about you in particular, and if so ask them what they noticed that gave them that impression. If it was something you said or did, listen to what they have to say. That is information where you have the choice to do with it what you want.
4. Notice the opportunity to let that person have their opinion without having to defend yourself.
5. Let the comment tickle you into laughing at yourself. If you can't make fun of yourself you are taking life too seriously.

Cf

Confident
[**kon**-fi-d*uh*nt]

1. having strong belief or full assurance
2. sure of oneself; having no uncertainty about one's own abilities, correctness,
3. successfulness, etc.; self-confident; bold

RECOGNIZE
YOUR THOUGHTS, FEELINGS & ENERGY

1. "I may not be sure of how I will do this but I know I will."
2. "Yes, of course I can."
3. "I know my way through this."
4. "I have handled this type of situation many times before."
5. "This is the right way forward."

You feel grounded, present and in touch with what is going on. You are mentally and emotionally calm and assured.

REALIZE
WHAT IS DRIVING YOUR MINDSET

1. You are in touch with your positive qualities. You have a positive view of yourself and while you know that you're not perfect, you feel good about your accomplishments and your capabilities.
2. You're thinking, "I got this," but it's not from arrogance.
3. You're very open, you're very transparent, you're humble. You are simply being very factual, you're being very supportive, and you take yourself lightly so you have a sense of humor.
4. Your confidence inspires people into their own confidence.
5. You know that you can do, you can perform, and there's a sense of ease, a sense of grace.
6. You have a view of yourself that matches other people's perception of you.

RESOLVE
TO BALANCE YOUR STRENGTHS

1. Create a plan and follow through until it's complete.
2. Know what you know and what you don't know. Ask for feedback and input on a regular basis.
3. Communicate your goals and process to others.
4. Acknowledge other ways of doing a task that you know how to do well.
5. Be curious when it appears that someone opposes you.
6. Help others acknowledge their value.
7. Maintain a high level of engagement throughout the work cycle.

CHECK YOUR TUDE ®

Jg

Judgmental

[juhj-**men**-tl]

1. attempts to gain power by assuming a superior position and insisting that others agree to maintain your self-righteousness
2. looking for and finding fault; a way of making oneself feel better by hurting others
3. is a proactive defense from the fear of being inadequate

RECOGNIZE
YOUR THOUGHTS, FEELINGS & ENERGY

1. "That was stupid."
2. "I will never amount to much."
3. "I can never get it right."
4. "You don't have what it takes."
5. "You are so ignorant I can't believe it."

You feel justified in your negative impressions of others. You place yourself in a one-up or one-down position.

REALIZE
WHAT IS DRIVING YOUR MINDSET

1. You think your perception is the truth about the situation, but really you have a monumental blind spot. You are not seeing the person or situation as it is but only your perception of it.
2. You have a blanket condemnation of the other person or situation that creates negativity for you and the other.
3. You have the illusion of feeling good about yourself but it is at the cost of making other people wrong.
4. You as the judger are the recipient of the judgment – you are eroding your own confidence and self-worth.
5. You are trying to stay safe from having to experience any intrusion into your weak self concept.
6. You keep the illusion of control by putting things in boxes with labels.
7. You are unwilling to accept or tolerate any perceived imperfection.

RESOLVE
TO MOVE FORWARD

1. Notice what happens if you accept the person or situation as it is.
2. Step into the shoes of the other. What might be their experience? How are they trying to win? What do they need to be successful? How could you support their success?
3. Notice you are judging yourself in the same way you are judging the other person or situation. What is it about yourself that is deserving or not about that judgment?
   • When did you begin having this attitude toward yourself?
   • Where did you learn how to judge yourself in this way?
4. Love yourself and stop being so harsh. Reclaim your initial state of innocence, openness and purity – sounds stupid, I know, but try it! Try something NEW – I dare you.

Accepting

[ək'sept ng]

1. recognize something for what it is
2. to believe the goodness, realness of something
3. to receive or answer affirmatively
4. something everyone in the world needs to do a lot more of – Urban Dictionary

RECOGNIZE
YOUR THOUGHTS, FEELINGS & ENERGY

1. "Not exactly what I wanted, but it is our starting point."
2. "We have some work to do."
3. "It could be a lot worse."
4. "This is just fine as it is."
5. "Not perfect, but it will do just fine."

You see fully what you have to work with and decide to make it work. You feel momentum for the work ahead.

REALIZE
WHAT IS DRIVING YOUR MINDSET

1. You want to work with the truth of what is, not what you think should be.

2. You are willing to work with what is in front of you as-is.

3. Your reaction to the gap between the way that would be ideal and the way things are is to engage and move forward.

4. You may not love it but you are going to work with it.

5. You know that nothing can be done to change what has happened or what is before you.

6. You are NOT resigned; you see a future.

7. True acceptance sounds easy. The challenge is to still your sense of urgency and not to want to change things immediately.

8. If you experience resistance, you are probably using force.

9. Assuming positive intention begins with acceptance.

10. The glass is neither half full nor half empty, it's just a glass with liquid.

RESOLVE
TO BALANCE YOUR STRENGTHS

1. Let people know you see the total picture of them and that you want to work with them.

2. Be the role model of acceptance. When they put themselves down, follow it with a positive that you authentically see.

3. Bring the goals into focus along with an action plan.

4. Listen to your internal commentary and transform judgments into encouragements.

5. For every judgment, think of an appreciation.

6. Bring in a sense of humor.

7. Get creative with how you will more forward.

8. Keep a forward momentum without being pushy.

9. Keep your eyes on the big picture of where you are going and appreciate the journey.

Web and App

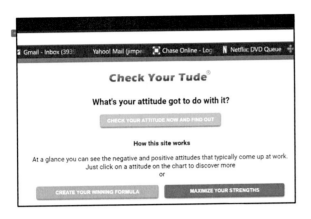

CHECK YOUR ATTITUDE NOW TO FIND OUT

Chart and information on Recognizing, Realizing and Resolving

CREATE YOUR WINNING FORMULA

The Winning Formula is a neuro-science program that helps you enhance your ability to change and transform your negative attitudes to positive attitudes. It gives you a chance to get familiar with the chart and your own attitude patterns.
5 rounds and will calculate your top strength.

MAXIMIZE YOUR STRENGTHS

The Maximize Your Strengths is a neuro-science program that helps you enhance your ability to change and transform your negative attitudes to positive attitudes. It gives you a chance to get familiar with the chart and your own attitude patterns.
10 rounds and will calculate the rank order of your 4 top strengths and tips on how to balance your strengths.

Check Your Tude®

		Negative Intention Shadows				Choice		Positive Intention Strengths		
Sb Sabotage										**Sv** Service
Vt Victim	**Re** Resigned	**Sp** Suspicious	**En** Envious	**Df** Defensive	**In** Inspired	**Cr** Creative	**Cu** Curious	**Cm** Committed		**Vi** Visionary
Ad Adversary	**Bl** Blaming	**Sr** Sarcastic	**Ag** Angry	**Fs** Frustrated	**Eg** Engaged	**Pa** Passionate	**Hu** Humorous	**Ac** Accountable		**Av** Activator
Rs Rescuer	**Su** Superior	**Cn** Controlling	**Ha** Hidden Agenda	**Ar** Arrogant	**Hm** Humble	**Tp** Transparent	**Tr** Trusting	**Sp** Supportive		**Co** Coach
Cy Cynic	**Sk** Skeptical	**Ct** Critical	**Is** Insulted	**Jg** Judgmental	**Ap** Accepting	**Cf** Confident	**Ob** Objective	**Md** Mindful		**Mn** Mentor

The Check Your Tude table is available as a customizable web application and e-learning platform that can run on your servers/remotely and provide mobile apps for your employees. We offer 3 levels of customization, licensing and training for your company.

Call or email for more information.

Jim Peal, Ph.D.

jim@peal.com

Tel. 805-966-3323

See Jim Peal on **TEDx** – "Decisions That Define Us"
Leadership, Team & Organizational Development
Books on Amazon
www.peal.com

Notes

· ·

· ·

· ·

· ·

· ·

· ·

· ·

· ·

· ·

· ·

· ·

· ·

Made in the USA
San Bernardino, CA
31 August 2016